Handmade
Beaded
Greetings Cards

Patricia Wing

SEARCH PRESS

First published in Great Britain 2005

Search Press Limited
Wellwood, North Farm Road,
Tunbridge Wells, Kent TN2 3DR

Reprinted 2006

ISBN10: 1 84448 059 3
ISBN 13: 978 84448 059 3

The Publishers and author can accept no responsibility for any consequences arising from the information, advice or instructions given in this publication.

Suppliers
If you have difficulty in obtaining any of the materials and equipment mentioned in this book, then please visit the Search Press website for details of suppliers:
www.searchpress.com

Alternatively, you can write to the Publishers at the address above for a current list of stockists, including firms who operate a mail-order service.

Publishers' note
All the step-by-step photographs in this book feature Patricia Wing's assistant, Ruth Venables, demonstrating how to make beaded cards. No models have been used.

Manufactured by Universal Graphics Pte Ltd, Singapore

Printed in Malaysia by Times Offset (M) Sdn Bhd

Special dedication
I would especially like to thank Ruth, a precious young lady, who kindly posed for all the step by step photographs and who, through her commitment and encouragement, has helped to make this book possible.

The Lord is my light and my salvation.
Psalm 27

Loving thanks to my husband Tony for all his help and advice, our son Andrew, daughter Louise and granddaughters Shannon and Tilley Rose.

ACKNOWLEDGEMENTS

Thanks to Roz Dace and Search Press for giving me this wonderful opportunity. Thanks also to:

Harrington's Nottingham Lace; Glitterati; 21st Century Beads and Impex, for beads; Anna Griffin, Erica Fortgens, Allnight Media and Dream Weaver for stencils; Avec Ornare for pricking templates; Hot off the Press for tag and envelope templates; Fiskars for paper edging and corner scissors; YLI for metallic threads and silk ribbon.

Cover
Beaded Gem Flowers

Pricked pale green parchment combined with gem flowers and delicate pearl beads are offset by gold and blue borders.

Page 1
Embellished Flower Centre

Punched flower shapes, pricking and embossing techniques were all used for this card, and flat-backed gems and beads were stuck on for a really striking effect.

Opposite
Beaded Bookmark

Stitched topaz beads with blue and amber gems were mounted on a cream laced border and finished with a gold tassel.

Contents

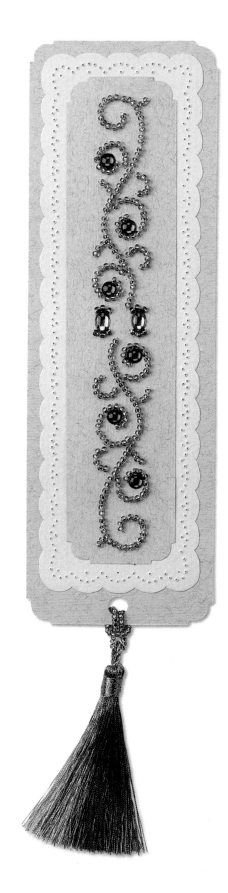

Introduction

There are so many techniques you can use for card making, and using beads, gems and lace with pricking and embossing techniques will considerably add to your repertoire.

There is a wealth of templates available for pricking out and stencils for embossing, to help create that extra special card. Most templates and stencils are a pleasure to work with, as someone has already created the design – you only have to follow the pattern, so pricking out or embossing could not be easier.

Stitching on beads adds another dimension, as do all the lovely gems. Beautiful lace will also complement the beadwork and you will be surprised at the originality you can achieve by cutting out designs from within the lace.

Although your cards will take longer to complete if you add these techniques, you will feel that the finished work is well worth all the effort. You can, of course, design your own beaded cards but pricking out the design first really helps with stitching on the beads.

The Victorians produced some extraordinarily beautiful cards, which form an important part of the heritage they bequeathed to us. Equally, the cards you create could become future family heirlooms that your family will cherish in years to come.

Keep an eye open for inexpensive jewellery – old earrings and brooches often have attractive glass gems that will enhance your work and make it unique. You can find all sorts of things in charity shops, and locally I visit an auction house where boxes of broken jewellery and oddments can yield a treasure-trove of embellishments for my cards!

Pat Wing

Opposite

These cards show some of the effects that can be created using beads, gems, pricking and embossing techniques and lace in your card making.

Materials

Templates and stencils

There is now huge range of templates for pricking and stencils for embossing available, which give you professionally designed patterns to use. The fun comes from selecting which parts of these designs you want to use to create your own unique work. Most embossing stencils are made from unpainted brass, whilst pricking templates are usually metal with a painted finish.

Envelope and tag templates are also very useful. They are made from flexible plastic and are transparent so that you can see where you are placing them on your card.

Pricking templates and embossing stencils shown with envelope and tag templates.

Tools

A cutting mat is a must, and those printed with a fine grid can be a great help when squaring or measuring card and paper. A craft knife and metal ruler are used for cutting card. Fancy-edged scissors are used to add decorative edges, as are corner scissors.

It goes without saying that your HB pencil must be kept sharp at all times for accurate work, so keep a sharpener to hand as well as an eraser.

Three sizes of embossing tool are sufficient to fit most stencils. When choosing a light box for embossing, go for one at least 20 x 30cm (8 x 12in), as this allows plenty of room to fix a stencil with tape and to rest your hand when working.

A pricking tool and pricking mat are used for pricking out designs.

A cocktail stick is used for picking up small gems.

Quilting needles in size 12 are most useful for stitching beads on to cards.

Use fine scissors for cutting out lace patterns and a pigment inkpad and dauber for dyeing them to your chosen colour. Kitchen paper is a must for keeping your work surface clean when colouring lace.

Craft punches are useful for punching out shapes to decorate your beaded cards. A single hole punch is used when adding tassels or ribbons to bookmarks or tags.

A metal ruler, pencil, eraser and sharpener, a light box, craft punches, a single hole punch, fancy-edged and corner scissors, a craft knife, needles, fine scissors, a cocktail stick, pricking and embossing tools, a pricking mat, pigment inkpad, dauber and kitchen paper, all on a cutting mat.

Sticky things

Low tack masking tape is used to stick your stencils or templates to the light box or to card, as it can easily be removed. Double-sided tape is very useful for layering card and the finger lift variety is especially easy to use. Small 3D foam squares are ideal for giving a three-dimensional aspect to your work. A fine-tipped PVA glue applicator is useful for sticking small gems to your work.

Cards and papers

I often used ready-made card blanks and cut them down to the size required, which can be a real time-saver. You can of course always make up your own cards – the material needs to be quite firm especially if you are pricking out and stitching.

Pastel paper is ideal for embossing and stitching but as it is only 160gsm (90lb), it needs to be applied to a firmer card so that it will stand up.

Parchment is an extremely versatile material as it can be used for embossing and stitching, it will readily accept colour, it can be made into flowers or used as inserts and it comes in a huge range of colours.

Card, pastel paper and parchment in a range of colours.

Beads, lace and other embellishments

There is such an array of beautiful coloured beads that come in all shapes and sizes. It is a pleasure to work with beads: they really do enhance one's cards. You can stitch them or glue them on.

There is also a stunning collection of cabouchons: flat-backed gems. They are made from glass or acrylic and are faceted or smooth. Imitation cameos also work well with beads. Imitation pearls come in an assortment of colours and shapes, also flat-backed.

Just studying the various intricate designs worked in lace will inspire you. Bridal motifs along with your beads and gems make stunning wedding cards.

There is an abundance of coloured threads which have many applications – stitching decorative borders is just one. Silk ribbons can be worked into the designs not only for cards but also for bookmarks and gift tags.

Beads, gems, imitation pearls, silk ribbon, thread, an imitation cameo and lace, all used to decorate cards.

Basic techniques

The techniques used to make the cards in this book, such as embossing and pricking, are easy to learn and perfect for beginners. You will be amazed at the beautiful cards you can make with a few simple techniques.

Punching shapes

Craft punches are a fantastic asset to card making – you just punch out the pattern, which could not be easier. Often you can choose to layer the shapes as punch patterns come in several different sizes.

1. Place the paper in the punch.

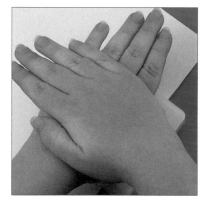

2. Press down firmly to cut through the paper.

3. The punched paper falls out underneath the punch.

Craft punches come in all shapes and sizes, and as shown here you can often punch the same shape in several sizes.

Pricking out

When pricking out to give a decorative pattern, the finished design can have a flat or a raised finish. These are achieved by pricking through your card either from the front (flat) or the reverse (raised).

1. Tape the template to the back of the card using masking tape. Pricking from the back creates a raised effect.

2. On a mat, use a pricking tool to prick through the holes in the template.

3. Peel off the tape and turn the card over to reveal the pattern.

The same design pricked from the front gives a flatter, softer effect.

Gluing on beads or gems

A fine-tipped PVA glue applicator makes it very easy to apply the smaller gems to your work – there is nothing worse than surplus glue!

1. Use a fine-tipped PVA glue applicator to place dots of glue where required.

2. Use a cocktail stick with a tiny bit of glue on the end to pick up a gem and place it on a glue dot on the design.

3. Press the gem with the other end of the cocktail stick to secure it.

The finished design.

Embossing with a light box

Embossing is done from the back of the card with a rounded tool which pushes the card into the pattern of the stencil. This gives an elegant, raised finish on the front of the card.

1. Using masking tape, fix the stencil to the centre of the light box. Switch on the light.

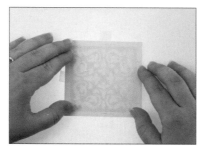

2. Tape the card over the stencil, right side down.

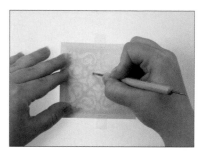

3. Press the embossing tool into the pattern as required.

4. You can select all or only part of the stencil pattern to suit your card design. When it is finished, peel off the tape and turn the card over to see the design.

Sewing on beads

This technique requires the template to be taped to the face of the card to give a flat finish, and you only need to prick through very lightly as a guide for the beading needle. It is best to use thread close in colour to the background of the card.

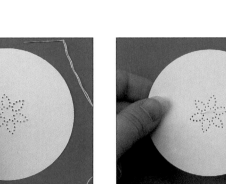

1. Lightly prick out the pattern using a pricking tool.

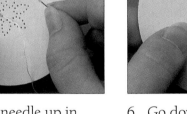

2. Tape the end of the thread to the back of the card.

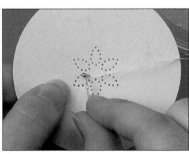

3. Bring the thread through hole 2 and pick up a bead on your needle.

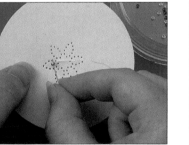

4. Secure the bead by going down hole 1.

5. Bring the needle up in hole 3 and pick up another bead.

6. Go down in hole 2.

7. Move on to the next group of three holes and continue in the same way to finish the design. Secure the end of the thread at the back with tape as you did at the start.

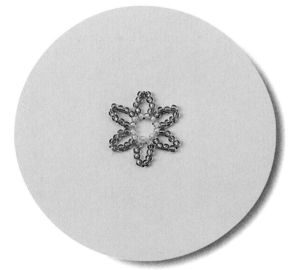

Folding card

You may want to make your own cards. A cutting mat can be used to centre the fold of your card, or you can measure and mark the card. Whichever way you choose, accuracy is very important.

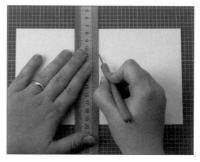

1. Mark the centre of the card with a pencil on the top and bottom edge, using the grid on your cutting mat as a guide.

2. Line up the ruler with the marks and score the card with a small embossing tool.

3. Fold along the scored line.

Making a border

1. To make a fine border, stick the design on to to a larger piece of coloured paper using double-sided tape.

2. Use the grid on your cutting mat to measure the width of the border, and trim the paper using a ruler and craft knife.

3. Cut the other three sides to the same width, using the grid as a guide.

Tip
Take your time when trimming to ensure a neat cut.

Making gem flowers

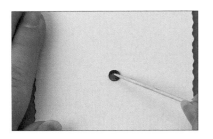

1. Glue the gem for the flower centre on to paper, as shown on page 11.

2. Use a fine-tipped PVA glue applicator to place a circle of glue around the gem.

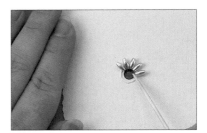

3. Use a cocktail stick to place oval pearls around the gem, pressing down towards the centre of the flower.

4. When the glue is dry, trim the paper away.

Dyeing lace

This technique allows you to colour pieces of lace the exact shade you need to match or complement your other embellishments. Here I use a pigment inkpad and a dauber.

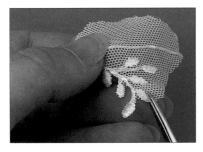

1. Cut out the part of the lace using fine scissors.

2. Place it on kitchen paper to keep your work surface clean. Tap the dauber on to the pigment ink pad.

3. Transfer the colour to the lace by tapping with the dauber. Leave to dry.

The finished dyed lace.

Pearl Daisies

A good starter card using pricking and gem gluing techniques. A basic lightly textured ivory card blank is decorated with pearl droplets and lilac gems and set off with a lilac paper border. The design can be varied by using different colour schemes.

You will need

Ivory card blank, folded size
123 x 152mm (4⁷/₈ x 6in)

Insert paper, 80gsm (20lb)
same size

Pricking tool and mat

Pricking template PRO555

Lilac paper, 118 x 148mm
(4⁵/₈ x 5⁷/₈in)

Cream card, 110 x 80mm
(4³/₈ x 3¹/₈in)

Sixteen lilac gems, 3mm (¹/₈in)

Four lilac faceted gems,
5mm (³/₁₆in)

Twenty white oval pearls

Twenty lilac oval pearls

Fine-tipped PVA
glue applicator and
cocktail stick

Craft knife and cutting mat

Double-sided tape

Masking tape

1. Place the template on the back of the card so that the motif is in the corner. Tape it down.

2. Place the card on a pricking mat and prick through the holes.

16

3. Move the template to the next corner and repeat.

4. Continue with the other two corners.

5. Take the piece of cream card, line up the motif on the stencil at the top of the card and tape it down.

6. Prick the pattern, then move the template to the bottom of the card and repeat.

7. Line up the motif at the side of the card, and prick again. Repeat the other side.

8. Stick the pricked cream card on to the lilac paper using double-sided tape.

9. Trim the paper to leave a 5mm (³/₁₆in) border, using a craft knife and cutting mat.

10. Stick the lilac paper to the centre of the main pricked card blank using double-sided tape.

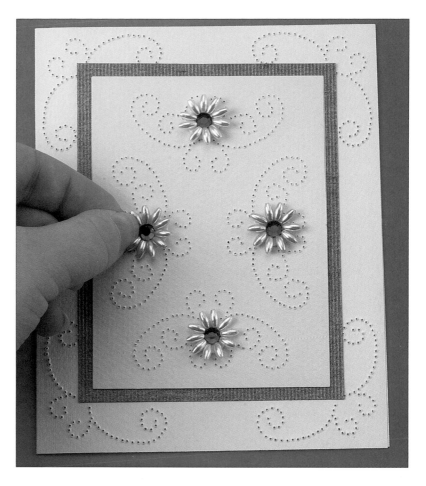

11. Make two white and two lilac daisies using the technique shown on page 15.

12. Stick the daisies in place as shown using PVA glue.

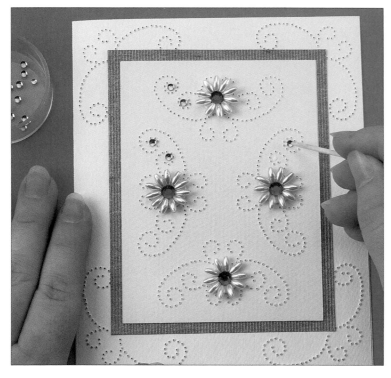

13. Use a fine-tipped PVA glue applicator to make dots of glue where the gems will go. Pick up gems using a cocktail stick with a little glue on the end and stick them in place.

Tip
For a professional
finish, always make an
insert for your card.

14. Fold the insert paper in half.

15. Open the card and stick the insert to the spine using dots of PVA glue from the applicator.

Opposite

The finished card. The pearl daisies set off the swirling pricked design perfectly and the purple gems and border make this a subtle yet striking card for any occasion.

Top: Two flowers were punched out and stuck to the centre as shown. I used pricking template PR0559 for pricking out the central circle, and embossed the circle containing the ring of amber beads using the same template. Bottom: The large green daisy sits on a scalloped punched shape. I wound gold thread round it and then used a 3D foam square to stick the shape on to a circle of green leaf parchment. The corners of the square card were embossed using stencil EF8004. The pricked out design comes from template PRO536. The embellishments are flat-backed gems.

Top: The white art deco wallet was made up using white marbled card. The technique shown on page 15 was used to make the daisy. I used pricking template PRO536 for the corners. Art Deco corner scissors give the decorative stepped effect. Bottom: stencil 5801S was used in various ways to create this card. Each corner of the card blank was embossed first, then the centre panel of the card, and finally the edge of the stencil was used to emboss the square shape, which was then mounted on to gold card.

Flowered Notecard

This card uses an original stitching pattern, the template for which is reproduced here actual size for you to photocopy. Cut out and dyed lace allows you to give the card a touch of originality.

You will need

Cream card blank, open size 130 x 300mm (5⅛ x 11¾in)

A4 card for template

Masking tape

A4 gold paper

Pricking tool and mat

Stamp design fancy-edged and fine scissors

Twelve amber and twelve ruby flat-backed teardrops

Two amber and two ruby faceted gems, 4mm (³⁄₁₆in)

One triangle gem

Leaf pattern lace

Green pigment inkpad and dauber

Green cotton embroidery thread

No. 12 quilting needle

Gold metallic thread

Fine-tipped PVA glue applicator and cocktail stick

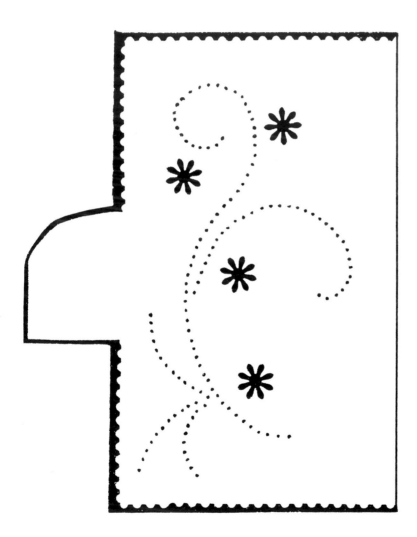

The pattern for the card's opening and for pricking, shown full size. Photocopy the pattern on to card and cut it out to make a template.

24

1. Place the card template at one end of your cream card as shown, and pencil round it to make the tab shape for the opening.

2. Score and fold the card as shown on page 14, 9cm (3½in) from the tab end and 6.5cm (2½in) from the other end. Cut to the pencil line using fancy-edged scissors, leaving the tab. Cut round the tab using ordinary scissors.

3. Tape the template to your cream card and prick the holes using a pricking tool and mat.

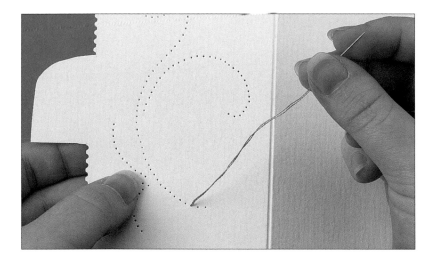

4. The stems are sewn in back stitch. Thread a needle and tape the end of the thread at the back of the card. Bring the needle up in hole 3 of the stem.

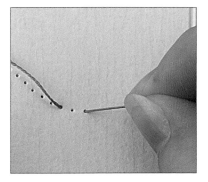

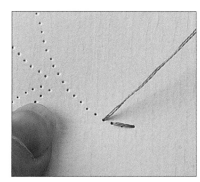

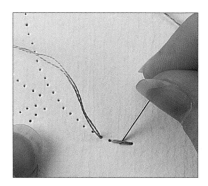

5. Take the needle down again in hole 1.

6. Bring the needle up in hole 4.

7. Put the needle down in hole 2.

8. When the green stem is complete, secure the gold thread at the back and bring the needle up in hole 1. Loop the gold thread through and over alternate green back stitches. Complete all the stems in the same way.

9. Cut out the leaves from the lace using fine scissors.

10. Dye the leaves green using an inkpad and dauber as shown on page 15.

11. Stick on the flower centre gems on using PVA glue and a cocktail stick.

12. Stick on the petals in the same way.

13. Use dots of PVA glue to stick on the dyed lace foliage.

 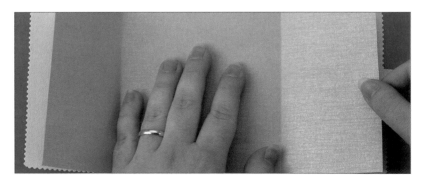

14. Use the template to cut a crescent of gold paper and stick it to the tab. Stick on the triangle gem.

15. Cut the gold paper to 242cm x 120mm (9½ x 4¾in) and score and fold it to match the card. Stick it in the card using dots of glue along the folds.

The finished card. Cutting and dyeing the lace for this card is easy to do and enhances the stitched stems to create an elegant and colourful design.

Top: Punch out four lilac 25mm (1in) squares and place them on a suitable square of white card. Prick tiny holes around the pattern thus formed and stitch through them with lilac thread. Stick on the gem flowers and finish by cutting out lace leaves. Place this panel on to a lilac parchment background before mounting it on to the base card.

Bottom: Emboss the card using stencil 5731S and very lightly pencil a lattice design using a ruler. Prick a tiny hole at the end of each line and stitch the lattice with gold thread. Fill the lattice squares with pearl seed beads and pink gems. Build the centre piece from a flat-backed pink oval with a surround of 2mm (¹/₁₆in) and 4mm (¹/₈in) gems. Mount the panel on to a finished card 125mm (5in) square.

Top: Place template PR0509 on to cream card and draw around the edge with pencil. Cut out the scallop shape and emboss the design twice from stencil 5731S. Place the template back on the card and prick out the pattern of holes required. Next, stitch the design in thread and finish by gluing on the gems. Finally mount on to green parchment and then on to the base card, size 125 x 160mm (5 x 6¼in).

Bottom: Using a large flower punch, produce a cream and a white flower and then emboss each with stencil 5819S. Mount the flowers on to a circle of pale green parchment. Emboss each corner of a 120mm (4¾in) square cream card. Using template PR0561, centre the card and prick out one hole at the edge of each internal scallop. Next bring the external scallop pattern to line up with these first two holes and prick out as shown, moving the template round each time. Prick one hole in the centre of each scallop before stitching with gold thread. Finally, place the flower head with the gem centre on to 3D foam squares to create a raised effect.

Cameo Card

This is a very simple card to produce using just two pricking templates, beads and thread. The subtle shades of the materials used give it an elegant, period feel. You can change the colours of the cameo and everything else to suit your personal taste.

You will need
A5 pink160gsm (90lb) pastel card

Cream card blank, folded size 124 x 162mm (4⁷⁄₈ x 6³⁄₈in)

Pricking templates PR0507 and PR0509

Pencil

Masking tape

Fine scissors

Needle and thread

Pearl seed beads

Pink cameo

Fine-tipped PVA glue applicator and cocktail stick

2mm (¹⁄₁₆in) pearl beads

Pricking tool and mat

3D foam squares

1. Tape the pricking template to the inside front of the cream card and begin pricking the design using a pricking tool and mat.

2. Finish pricking the border and close the cream card to reveal the design.

3. Tape the oval template on to the pink card, pencil round it and cut it out.

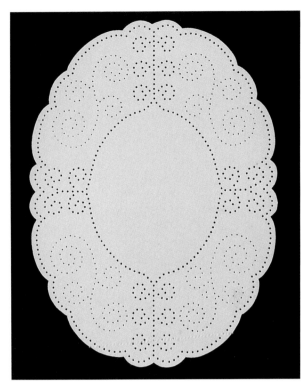

4. Prick part of the design using a pricking tool and mat.

5. Remove the template, turn the card over and prick the rest of the design from the other side to create a partly raised, partly flat pattern as shown.

6. Sew on the pearl seed beads using back stitch as shown on page 13.

7. Place 3D foam squares on the back of the pricked oval and peel off the backing.

8. Stick the oval down in the centre of the pricked cream card blank.

9. Stick the cameo in the centre of the card using PVA glue.

10. Glue a row of 2mm (¹⁄₁₆in) pearl beads around the edge of the cameo using PVA glue and a cocktail stick.

11. Use the fine-tipped PVA glue applicator to place tiny dots of glue outside the circle of pearls. Use a cocktail stick dipped in glue to pick up and place seed beads as shown.

The finished card shows the two styles of pricking: from the back, creating the raised border, and from the front, giving a softer look – a perfect base on which to sew beads for a neat yet stylish finish.

Top left: Draw round the edge of template PR0529 on pale green parchment, cut out the shape and prick out the raised design from the reverse. Mount this on to gold card and stick to a basic card 125 x 160mm (5 x 6¼in). Now place template PR0507 on the front of some ivory card and prick out part of the design as shown. Make the flowers by using template PR0558 to prick out the pattern and then stitching on pearl beads. Use tube beads for the stems and gems to complete the flowers. Mount the stitched design on to blue then gold cards leaving narrow borders showing and fix the gold card on to the pricked green parchment.

Bottom left: Using part of template PR0529, prick out to show the raised effect on the cream card. Emboss round the edge of the envelope template and cut this out. Use part of stencil 5802S to emboss the top flap. Finish with silk ribbon and gems.

Opposite, top: Take a cream 125mm (5in) square card blank and prick out the corners from the reverse to give the raised effect. Stick amber gems in each corner. Using template PR0536, first prick out the bottom half of the design and draw around the scallop edge, then turn the template and repeat this for the top half of the design before cutting out as shown. Place on to a circle of deep cream card. Next make up the centre flower using template PR0509, mount this on to a cream circle and embellish with the daisy.

Opposite, far right: The overall size of this bookmark is 60 x 185mm (2³⁄₈ x 7¼in). Start with a piece of blue/green card and a piece of cream card this size. Using template PR0509, prick out and scallop the edge of the cream card and stick this to the blue/green backing which has had the corners cut with corner scissors. Next cut the inner card, trim its corners and prick it using template PR0558 to take the beads and gems.

34

Purple Parchment

This simple but effective card uses template PR0558 and incorporates deep purple parchment and gems to complement the pricked patterns.

You will need

Cream card blank, folded size 122 x 170mm (4¾ x 6¾in)

Ivory 160gsm (90lb) pastel card, 120 x 150mm (4¾ x 5⅞in)

Fancy-edged scissors, cloud design

Pricking template PR0558

Masking tape

Pricking tool and mat

Deep purple parchment

Fine-tipped PVA glue applicator and cocktail stick

Pencil, craft knife, metal ruler and cutting mat

Crystal and purple teardrops

Crystal and purple 4mm (⅛in) flat-backed faceted gems

Double-sided tape

1. Secure the template to the back of the ivory card, making sure the design is central. Prick the central design.

2. Cut down the sides of the card to 100mm (4in) wide using fancy-edged scissors. Make sure the sides match.

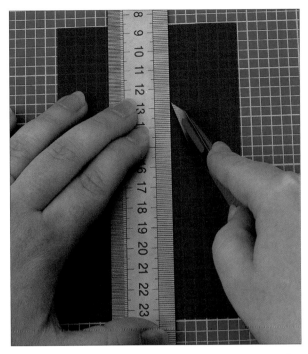

3. Measure, draw and cut out four pieces of purple parchment, 35 x 150mm (1⅜ x 5⅞in) using a craft knife, metal ruler and cutting mat.

4. Use the pricking tool and mat to prick the daisy border from the template on two of the strips of parchment. The raised side will show.

5. Put double-sided tape on one edge of the front of a plain strip of purple parchment.

6. Stick the cream scalloped card on top so that the purple parchment just shows from underneath. Repeat the other side.

7. Using a fine-tipped PVA glue applicator, place dots of glue in the pricked petal shapes on the parchment. Place teardrop gems on the dots to form petals.

8. Stick circular gems on to form the flower centres. Repeat with the other pricked parchment strip.

9. When the glue is dry, turn the parchment over and place a dot of glue behind each gem.

Tip
Gluing parchment to the card by applying glue behind the gems prevents the glue from showing through the parchment.

10. Stick the parchment strips to the main artwork as shown. Mount the artwork centrally on the cream card blank using double-sided tape.

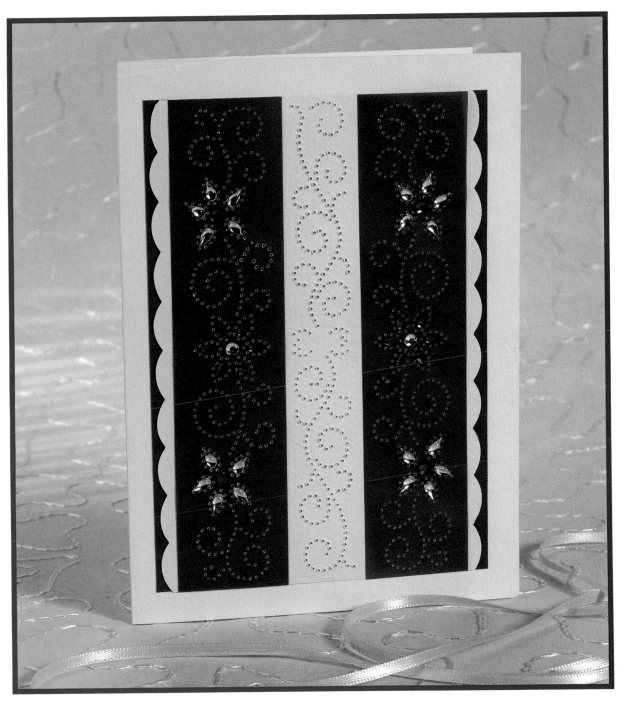

The finished card. The crystal gems are shown to their best advantage against the deep purple parchment. This is just one of many designs provided on template PR0558.

Top: This blue cameo card uses template PR0559 and a 120mm (4¾in) square card blank. I pricked out from the reverse side on two ivory 160gsm (90lb) pastel squares. I then mounted these on to pale blue parchment and decorated them with flat-backed faceted blue gems and pearls, surrounding the central blue cameo.

Bottom left: Here I cut out a gift tag blank using a template. I then pricked the blue panel in a lattice design with a decorative border, worked the lattice in thread, and glued on gem flowers.

Bottom right: For this bookmark, pink and ivory 160gsm (90lb) pastel paper was decorated in the same way as the main project card using PR0558 and mounted on purple parchment, which shows at the edges, with matching silk ribbons.

For this parchment fan, emboss around the top part of template PR0356 on to green parchment. Cut out the semi-circle and wind gold thread around the scallops from a hole made with a single hole punch as shown. Next, on cream parchment, emboss and cut out as before but then tape the template on to the front of the parchment and prick out the pattern, finishing with amber gems. Emboss the bottom part of the template on to another piece of cream parchment, cutting out, pricking and gluing amber teardrops as shown. Punch out a scallop-edged circle from green parchment, punch a central hole, cut it as shown and wind it with gold thread as for the larger semi-circle. Now assemble the four parts of the fan, finish with a gold tassel and place it on the cream card background embossed with window stencil LJ811.

Lilac and Lace

Lilac stitched beads and parchment blend together so well to complement a selected piece of white lace. The corners of the lightly textured card are embossed to add further elegance.

You will need

Light box

Cream card blank, folded size 120mm x 175mm (4¾ x 6⁷/₈in)

A5 cream card

Stencils 5802S and EF8013

Template PR0507

Masking tape

Lilac seed beads

Lilac parchment

Pricking tool and mat

Embossing tool

Pencil

Fine scissors

Piece of lace

Fine-tipped PVA glue applicator

Double-sided tape

1. Tape the embossing stencil on the light box.

2. Open the card blank and tape it in place as shown. Emboss the corner using the embossing tool. Emboss each of the other three corners in the same way.

The card with the four corners embossed.

3. Tape the stencil on the front of the card with the pricking out design in the corner, just inside the embossed design. Prick out the design in each corner, using a pricking tool and mat.

4. Sew on the beads as shown on page 13.

5. Using the same pricking out design on purple parchment, prick out the pattern four times.

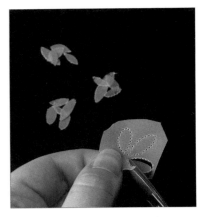

6. Using the prick marks as a guide, cut out teardrop shapes from the parchment.

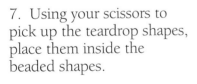

7. Using your scissors to pick up the teardrop shapes, place them inside the beaded shapes.

8. Apply masking tape to the parts of the oval template that will not be used.

9. Stick the stencil on to lilac parchment. Turn the parchment over and run the medium embossing tool around the top half of the template.

10. Realign the template ready to do the bottom half.

11. Run the embossing tool around the bottom half.

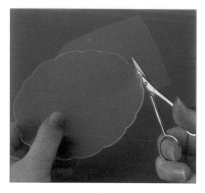

12. Remove the template and cut around the outside of the embossed line.

13. Stick the stencil to the A5 cream card and pencil round the top edge.

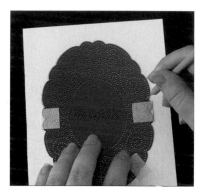

14. Prick the last hole on each side as shown.

15. Realign the template using the pricked holes as a guide and pencil around the bottom edge.

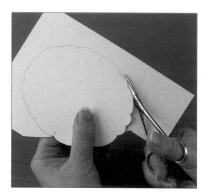

16. Cut out the shape.

17. Reapply the template and lightly prick the edge.

18. Stitch on lilac beads around the border as shown on page 13.

19. Cut out the lace motif.

20. Mount the lace on to lilac parchment using dots of glue behind heavy areas of lace. Trim away the edges.

21. Mount the lace and parchment on to the beaded cream card using double-sided tape.

22. Mount these on to the lilac parchment oval in the same way.

23. Mount the artwork on to the main card.

The finished card. Keeping to a simple colour scheme enhances this card, and putting the lace over the lilac parchment coordinates the overall design.

Top left: Use part of template PR0505 to prick out the basic pattern for stitching, then use the flower design in the corner of the template to make the two flowers in the centre of the card. Stitch the outline in pale turquoise and ivory beads before gluing the appropriate beads into the patterns. Cut out and stick on pale turquoise lace before adding the final bead embellishments.

Top right: Using template PR0554 for the centre and PR0559 for the corners, I have pricked out the simple but effective design you see stitched with pale yellow seed beads. Twelve large, pale, amber flat-backed teardrops are glued on and cut-out lace is repeated in the four corners. The central lace flower has been enhanced with tiny pale yellow beads.

Bottom left: Template PR0558 is used to prick out raised patterns at the sides and a flat pattern for stitching on beads in the centre. Two strips of white lace backed with pink parchment are then laid between the patterns.

Bottom right: The square card has embossed corners from stencil 5802S. The design is pricked out from template PR0536 after first embossing the edge of the template in to the card. Pale amber seed beads are stitched on, flat-backed pearls are added and the white seed beads are glued into the amber patterns. The lace is added last.

Index

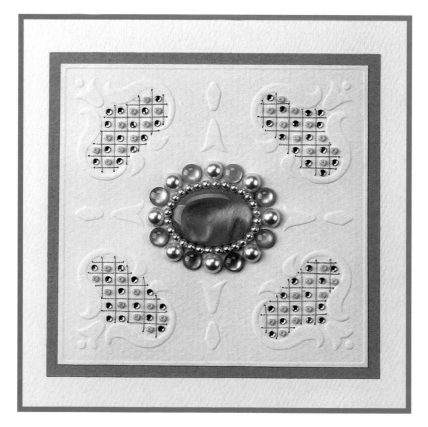

The central panel of this card was embossed. The lattice designs were very lightly drawn on, then pricked and stitched using gold thread. The central pink oval gem is surrounded by pink and pearl gems, and tiny seed beads and gems also decorate the lattice patterns.